Original title:
Love's Symphony

Copyright © 2024 Swan Charm
All rights reserved.

Author: Olivia Orav
ISBN HARDBACK: 978-9916-89-187-2
ISBN PAPERBACK: 978-9916-89-188-9
ISBN EBOOK: 978-9916-89-189-6

Melodies of Affection

In the silence, hearts entwine,
Soft whispers dance like vines.
Fingers trace the starlit air,
Love's sweet song finds us there.

Through the night, dreams take flight,
Holding close, in warm light.
Echoes of laughter cascade,
In this serenade, love is made.

Gentle breezes carry our vows,
Underneath the moonlit brows.
Each note strums a gentle chord,
Melodies that can't be ignored.

Time stands still, moments freeze,
Every glance, a gentle tease.
In this symphony, we belong,
Together we write love's song.

Ballad of the Beating Heart

With every thump, a story's told,
In rhythm, our destinies unfold.
Two souls moving in perfect tune,
Under the watchful gaze of the moon.

In shadows deep, fear takes flight,
With each pulse, we embrace the night.
Whispers soft, a promise made,
In the quiet, love won't fade.

Heartbeat echoes, a deep refrain,
In passion's fire, we feel no pain.
Through storms and trials, we won't part,
Together we sing our ballad's heart.

Amid the chaos, we find our peace,
In every sigh, a sweet release.
Close your eyes, feel the spark,
Guided by our beating hearts.

Crescendo of Connection

Two paths converge, a sacred space,
In every glance, love finds its place.
Notes of laughter swell and rise,
In harmony, our spirits fly.

With every touch, the crescendo grows,
In this symphony, our love flows.
Wrapped in warmth, the world fades,
In tender moments, love cascades.

Close your eyes, feel the beat,
In every heartbeat, life's sweet sheet.
Together we climb, hand in hand,
In this crescendo, love takes a stand.

Each laughter shared, a note of cheer,
Together we sing, forever near.
With every breath, our hearts expand,
Creating a melody, perfectly planned.

Dance of Tenderness

In twilight's glow, we take the floor,
In sweet rhythm, we share more.
With every step, our hearts align,
In this dance, we softly shine.

Gentle sways and lingering glances,
In your arms, my spirit dances.
A slow embrace, time draws near,
In this waltz, love's sweet cheer.

Through soft whispers and shared smiles,
We waltz along through endless miles.
Every touch, a feather's grace,
In this tenderness, we find our place.

So let the music play tonight,
In this dance, we find our light.
With every heartbeat, pulse in time,
Together we move, our love's sweet rhyme.

The Sweetest Refrain

In the morning light we dance,
With whispers soft and sweet.
Memories twirl, lost in trance,
Life's melody in heartbeat.

A gentle breeze through the trees,
Carries notes of love so pure.
In every sigh, in every breeze,
The sweetest thoughts we endure.

Stars above our heads align,
Every glimmer tells a story.
In each moment, love will shine,
A symphony of glory.

Hands entwined, we find our way,
Through the trials, through the fear.
We'll sing out loud, come what may,
Together, always near.

With every beat, our hearts combine,
In perfect harmony we play.
The sweetest refrain intertwines,
In love's embrace, we sway.

Chorus of Cherished Moments

In laughter shared, our spirits soar,
Each memory a treasured song.
With every glance, we seek for more,
In the dance where we belong.

Sunsets painted in gold hue,
As shadows stretch and intertwine.
Every heartbeat whispers true,
A chorus bright, both yours and mine.

With every hug, the world falls still,
Time pauses, holding gentle grace.
In each embrace, we find the thrill,
Of cherished moments we can trace.

In quiet nights, as stars awake,
We find our dreams, entwined in light.
For every step that we do take,
Our hearts beat strong, in love's sweet flight.

Together, we create the sound,
Of whispered hopes and dreams to share.
In every note, joy can be found,
In this chorus, two hearts laid bare.

Timeless Crescendo

As seasons change, our love remains,
A song that never fades away.
In joyful chords, through joy and pains,
We find the truth in words we say.

With every note, we climb so high,
No mountain steep can hold us down.
In every laugh, on every sigh,
A timeless tale of love's renown.

Hand in hand, we face the storm,
A melody that washes over.
In your embrace, I feel so warm,
As the world fades, we sing forever.

Together, let the music play,
With rhythms strong and spirits free.
In perfect harmony, we'll stay,
In timeless crescendos, you and me.

In the depths of night, we glow bright,
With dreams that soar beyond the dawn.
Our hearts in sync as stars ignite,
In love's embrace, we're never gone.

A Tuning of Two Hearts

In the silence, we align,
Two souls in sweet unison.
With gentle whispers, love we'll find,
In every moment, we are one.

The tuning forks of fate we blend,
Creating music, rich and true.
With every beat, my heart will mend,
In this duet, I choose you.

The world may spin, the tides may turn,
But in your eyes, the light I see.
With every flame, my heart will burn,
In our symphony, we are free.

Through ups and downs, we'll find our way,
With every challenge faced as one.
In perfect tune, love will relay,
Our melody, a rising sun.

In this dance, our spirits soar,
An orchestra of dreams and grace.
Two hearts in concert, evermore,
In sweet harmony, we embrace.

Prelude to Forever

In twilight's gentle glow, we stand,
Two souls entwined, hand in hand.
Promises whispered on the breeze,
A love that bends, but never flees.

Each heartbeat sings a sweet refrain,
Two lovers dance through joy and pain.
The world fades with each stolen glance,
In this moment, we dare to chance.

Through storms and trials we will soar,
Together building dreams galore.
The stars above our guiding light,
In shadows deep, we find our sight.

As time unfolds its tender lace,
We carve our names in cosmic space.
For every whisper, every sigh,
A prelude penned beneath the sky.

This journey blooms, with passion bright,
A saga formed in pure delight.
With every dawn, love's promise grows,
In harmony where true love flows.

The Aria of Affection

A melody soft in the night's embrace,
Sings of a love time cannot erase.
With every note, our spirits soar,
In an aria crafted forevermore.

Your laughter dances like summer rain,
Washing away each corner of pain.
A serenade wrapped in trust so deep,
In this lullaby, our hearts will leap.

From dusk to dawn, the music plays,
Carving our memories in timeless ways.
Each chord a promise, each lyric a dream,
In this love song, together we gleam.

When shadows stretch and darkness falls,
The sweet refrain forever calls.
Hold me close, as we sing in tune,
Under the watchful eye of the moon.

Together we'll write our symphony,
In perfect harmony, just you and me.
In every heartbeat, the music swells,
An aria that time forever tells.

Harmony of Hearts

In quiet whispers, our hearts align,
A sacred bond, a love divine.
With every touch, a gentle spark,
Together lighting up the dark.

The world's chaos fades away,
In your embrace, I long to stay.
With every heartbeat, we create,
A melody that won't abate.

Through fields of gold, we wander free,
In every moment, just you and me.
Nature's chorus sings our bliss,
In harmony found in every kiss.

As seasons change and years go by,
Our love will write the endless sky.
In symphonic waves, we drift and flow,
As two entwined, forever grow.

With each sunrise, our song will play,
A timeless dance that won't decay.
In harmony, we'll find our ways,
Together through all our coming days.

Serenade of Souls

In the soft glow of twilight's embrace,
Two souls converge in a sacred space.
With each heartbeat, a story unfolds,
A serenade whispered, secrets told.

In moonlit nights, we share our dreams,
A tapestry woven with love's soft gleams.
Your laughter dances on evening air,
A melody sweet, beyond compare.

Through life's journey, hand in hand,
Together we forge a love so grand.
In every challenge, together we stand,
A serenade written on life's strand.

When dusk descends, and shadows creep,
In your arms is where I find sleep.
With every sigh, our spirits unite,
In this serenade, pure and bright.

As stars begin to twinkle and shine,
Know that forever, you will be mine.
In every note, our hearts will thrive,
In the serenade of souls alive.

The Harmonization of Hearts

Two souls entwined, in dance they sway,
    Silent whispers guide the way.
    A gentle touch, a fragile spark,
    Love's melody fills the dark.

    In the twilight's warm embrace,
    Harmony finds its rightful place.
    Notes collide, and hearts align,
    In this moment, love does shine.

    Seasons change, yet still they sing,
    The joy that true love can bring.
    Hand in hand, through thick and thin,
    Together they shall always win.

Through laughter's song and sorrow's tune,
  Each heartbeat sways beneath the moon.
    Every glance a sacred art,
    In the symphony of heart.

    As echoes linger, vows remain,
    In every joy and every pain.
  With every breath, they craft their part,
    In the harmonization of the heart.

Instrumentals of Infinity

In a universe vast and grand,
Cosmic rhythms walk the land.
Stars collide in vibrant shows,
Echoing through the night that glows.

Time creates its endless score,
Each moment opening a door.
The symphony unfolds in space,
A harmony we all embrace.

Galaxies twirl in endless dance,
In their spirals, we find our chance.
To play our notes, to join the flow,
In this timeless cosmic show.

Softly strumming, the planets sing,
To the tune of everything.
Beyond the veil of what we see,
These instrumentals set us free.

In the silence, secrets dwell,
Each heartbeat a story to tell.
With every glance at stars above,
We find the rhythm of our love.

The Unwritten Score

Pages blank, awaiting dreams,
Ink flows gently, or so it seems.
Every note a tale untold,
In quiet whispers, hopes unfold.

Fingers poised upon the keys,
Dancing lightly with the breeze.
A melody escaping fate,
In the silence, we create.

Brush and pen, the world's design,
Crafting moments, yours and mine.
Each heartbeat forms the written word,
In this symphony, love's absurd.

Harmonies linger, shadows play,
Catch the music of the day.
Life unscripted, wild and free,
In our hearts, the melody.

Finding solace in the muse,
Every choice, we gladly choose.
In the spaces where we soar,
Lies the beauty of unwritten score.

Resting in Rhythms

In the hush of twilight's gleam,
We find peace in the dream.
Gentle tides of night invite,
Quiet whispers, soft and light.

Nestled deep in twilight's arms,
Echoing the world's charms.
With every breath, our spirits sway,
In the twilight's gentle play.

Time slows down, the world a blur,
In this moment, we concur.
As stars blanket the night sky,
We let go, together we fly.

Resting deep in nature's hold,
Every heartbeat, a story told.
With every sigh, we feel it rise,
The rhythm of the tranquil skies.

In the dawn's embrace, we wake,
To the music, hearts may break.
But here we rest, our spirits flow,
In the rhythm of love, we glow.

Melodies in Moonlight

Under the silver glow, whispers dance,
Echoes of dreams in a twilight trance.
Stars wink above, secrets they share,
Harmony floats in the cool night air.

Leaves sway gently, a melodic sigh,
Night's lullaby makes the shadows lie.
With every note, the heart takes flight,
Wrapped in the magic of soft moonlight.

A river glimmers, reflecting the song,
Nature's chorus, where we all belong.
Dreamers unite, lost in the sound,
In melodies found, true peace unbound.

Every sigh sings of love's embrace,
In the stillness, we find our place.
The world fades, just you and I,
In moonlit moments, we learn to fly.

As dawn approaches, the melodies fade,
Yet in our hearts, the song is laid.
Carry the whispers into the day,
Where memories linger, and dreams won't stray.

Vibrato of Vulnerability

In the depths of silence, fears reside,
Fragile chords, emotions collide.
A trembling heart, with stories to tell,
Sings softly of wounds, woven so well.

Bare souls exposed, longing for light,
Dancing in shadows, embracing the night.
Each quiver a truth, raw and profound,
In harmony found, we're finally unbound.

With every note, horizons enlarge,
Strength emerges, like waves at charge.
Vulnerability, a powerful song,
In the fire of courage, we all belong.

As we sing out, the walls start to fall,
Together we rise, together we call.
In the vibrato, we share our pain,
Creating a symphony, love in the rain.

And when the echoes begin to subside,
We find our peace, no need to hide.
For in each tremor, we learn to trust,
Vibrato of hearts, a bond that's a must.

Serenading the Silence

In the hush of dusk, a soft tune plays,
Filling the void with gentle delays.
Whispers of stillness paint the air,
Serenades linger, magic laid bare.

A sigh of relief, a world stands still,
With each breath shared, the heart we will.
Moments elongate, a cherished embrace,
In silence, we find our sacred space.

The melody swells, drawing us near,
In the quiet, our truths appear.
No need for words, let the stillness sing,
In harmony found, love takes wing.

Crickets join in, a rhythmic hum,
Nature's soft choir calls us to come.
With every note, we learn to listen,
In serenades deep, our souls glisten.

As night unfolds, and stars burst to life,
We dance through shadows, free of strife.
Serenading the silence, our hearts align,
In this tranquil calm, forever entwined.

Staccato Moments

Time ticks quickly, sharp and bright,
In staccato beats, we chase the light.
Every glance a flash, a fleeting chance,
Life's rhythm calls us to dance.

Sudden laughter cuts through the air,
Pulse of joy, a sweet affair.
Each moment a spark, vibrant and clear,
In staccato bursts, we draw near.

Chasing echoes, we dart and dash,
In vibrant hues, memories flash.
A heartbeat races, life on the run,
Collecting moments, one by one.

In between pauses, time holds its breath,
Every second counts, life's quiet depth.
Hold it close, the beauty in haste,
Staccato moments, never to waste.

As dawn breaks, the tempo slows,
In the stillness, the heart knows.
For in each burst, we truly live,
In staccato moments, love will give.

Chords of Desire

In twilight's glow, we find our tune,
Soft whispers dance beneath the moon.
Hearts entwined in gentle grace,
Each note a sigh, each glance in place.

Held close within, our secrets sealed,\nIn harmony, our fate revealed.
With every strum, the passion grows,
A serenade only we know.

Beneath the stars, our voices blend,
In melodies, our souls descend.
The world fades away, just us two,
In chords of love, forever true.

The silence speaks of dreams untold,
In softest hues, our lives unfold.
With every heartbeat, we compose,
The sweetest song that love bestows.

As the night wanes, the echoes stay,
In vibrant chords, they softly play.
Together, bound by music's fire,
In every breath, the chords of desire.

Strings of Connection

Across the night, a thread of sound,
In whispers shared, our souls are found.
Each heartbeat tees, a pulse refined,
A symphony of hearts entwined.

In laughter shared and tears that flow,
The music sparks, our spirits grow.
With gentle pull, the strings align,
A tapestry of love's design.

Through every storm, we face the light,
In shadows deep, you are my sight.
Together played, our lives compose,
A melody that ever flows.

In quiet moments, hand in hand,
The world dissolves, we understand.
With every note, a bridge we build,
In heart's embrace, our dreams fulfilled.

So as we weave our lives anew,
In every chord, I'll stay with you.
In endless dance, our souls connect,
In strings of love, we find respect.

The Music of Affection

In soft arise, the dawn unfolds,
With every glance, a story told.
Through gentle notes, emotions swell,
In every heartbeat, love's great spell.

The rhythm formed in quiet sighs,
In whispered dreams and starlit skies.
Each moment shared a precious tune,
Creating music, hearts attune.

With every laugh, our spirits rise,
In sweetness found, the heart complies.
The songs we share, a bond so deep,
In life's embrace, our love we keep.

In vibrant hues, our colors blend,
In harmony, our hearts transcend.
With every dance, the truth we find,
In music's grace, our souls aligned.

So let the world around us fade,
In notes of love, we are not afraid.
In every chord, affection sings,
A melody that eternal brings.

Rhythmic Reflections

In shadows cast, reflections gleam,
Within our dance, we weave a dream.
The rhythm's pulse, a guiding light,
In every step, we take our flight.

With curious glances, eyes convey,
The secrets held in night and day.
In every sway, our spirits tell,
The stories deep, we know so well.

The echoes of what once has been,
In rhythmic flows, we delve within.
In whispered thoughts and silent streams,
We find our truths amidst our dreams.

As tides will change, our song remains,
Through joy and sorrow, loss and gains.
With every beat, the heart reflects,
In love's embrace, our path connects.

So let the rhythms guide our way,
In every note, we find our play.
In reflections deep, our love's refrain,
Forever bound, through joy and pain.

Crescendo of the Unseen

In shadows deep, the whispers rise,
A symphony where silence lies.
Hidden chords in twilight's grace,
Echoing dreams in time and space.

Unseen hands play the fragile strings,
Creating worlds where stillness sings.
Every note, a heartbeat shared,
A tapestry of moments dared.

As colors collide in moonlit night,
A dance of forces, pure and bright.
With each crescendo, secrets bloom,
Awakening life from the depths of gloom.

In this realm, the unseen flows,
A river where the spirit goes.
Treading softly on the breeze,
Finding solace in melodies free.

So let the music guide your way,
Through darkest nights and brightest day.
For in the silence, love resides,
In the crescendo, the heart confides.

The Heart's Playlist

In tangled wires, emotions play,
A playlist spun with joy and sway.
Each song a moment, soft and bright,
   Carving echoes in the night.

From laughter shared to whispered fears,
Every beat, a tale that steers.
Melodies of love, woven strong,
A symphony where we belong.

The rhythm of longing, a tender sigh,
Underneath the vast, starlit sky.
Notes of warmth that gently unfold,
Capturing memories, rich and bold.

In every chorus, hopes revive,
A celebration of being alive.
As the heart dances to the beat,
Life unfolds in moments sweet.

So play the songs that speak your truth,
Embrace the echoes of your youth.
For in this playlist, love's refrain,
The heart finds solace, again and again.

Notes of Nostalgia

In sepia tones, the memories gleam,
A gentle nod to a long-lost dream.
Each note a whisper of yesteryears,
Carried softly through laughter and tears.

The piano plays where shadows dance,
Inviting echoes in a wistful trance.
Fleeting moments, like fireflies,
Illuminate nights under endless skies.

With every chord, the past awakes,
Revealing paths that time forsakes.
A melody sewn in tender threads,
Where hope ignites as the sorrow sheds.

Notes of nostalgia wrap around,
Binding hearts where love is found.
In every pause, a heartbeat waits,
A fragrance sweet that time creates.

So let the music take its flight,
Through twilight hues and morning light.
For in these notes, the past resides,
In harmony where memory abides.

A Journey in Melodies

With every step, the music flows,
Guiding paths where freedom grows.
A journey traced on whispered air,
Each note a compass, bright and rare.

Through valleys deep and mountains tall,
The rhythm beckons, answering the call.
In every turn, a fresh refrain,
Carved in laughter, colored in pain.

With each measure, discover new lands,
A symphony crafted by unseen hands.
The beauty of sound in every breath,
Tales unfolding, life and death.

In the dance of sun and moon above,
We find the notes that speak of love.
So let us wander, hearts aligned,
In melodies timeless, endlessly entwined.

For every step we take in time,
Writes a story, a hopeful rhyme.
And as we journey, hand in hand,
The music of life, a glorious band.

Luminous Melodies

In twilight's glow, soft whispers play,
Bright notes arise at the close of day.
Each sound a spark, each chord a dream,
In this sweet night, they gleam and beam.

With every strum, a magic flow,
The heart beats strong, the tune will grow.
Dancing shadows, a serenade,
Eternal echoes, love displayed.

A gentle breeze carries the sound,
In the stillness, our hopes are found.
Feeling the warmth of every note,
A tide of joy, a vibrant boat.

Under starry skies, we unite,
Melodies soar, taking flight.
In harmony, our spirits blend,
Luminous dreams that never end.

Tuning into You

In every glance, a story shines,
Your laughter dances, like intertwining vines.
With open hearts, we find the tune,
A symphony beneath the moon.

Fingers touch, the world fades away,
Harmonies whisper what words can't say.
Together we craft a sweet refrain,
In your embrace, losses wane.

The rhythm pulses, a beating heart,
In perfect sync, we'll never part.
Your every smile, a note divine,
In the score of love, we intertwine.

Life's melody, it bends and sways,
With you, my love, it brightly plays.
Forever tuned, we sing our song,
In these moments, we belong.

Notes of Nostalgia

In sepia tones, memories reside,
Songs from the past, a cherished guide.
Each note a whisper, a ghostly call,
Echoes of laughter in shadowed halls.

The vinyl spins, a story unfolds,
Tales of love in the music, retold.
A fleeting moment, captured in time,
In every heartbeat, a perfect rhyme.

With every chord, the past replays,
Longing entwined in the softest haze.
In silence, we find a voice profound,
In every memory, a treasure found.

Though time moves on, we hold it dear,
In melodies played, you feel me near.
Nostalgic tunes like stars align,
Reminders of love, forever shine.

The Dance of Hearts

In a silent room, our spirits meet,
Twirls of emotion, so soft, so sweet.
With every step, our souls take flight,
Together we sway under waning light.

In this embrace, the world dissolves,
With rhythm and grace, our hearts evolve.
A fleeting moment, yet timeless too,
In the dance of hearts, it's me and you.

Whispers of love in every turn,
Candlelit dreams in our hearts that burn.
Lost in the music, we glide away,
In the dance of forever, we find our way.

Every glance, a stroke of art,
With each beat, we unravel part.
In this ballet, we share our fears,
The dance of hearts, where love adheres.

Sonata of Secrets

Whispers float in evening air,
Hidden truths, a silent dare.
Notes of shadows softly play,
Crafting dreams that fade away.

In the dark, our hearts entwine,
Every secret, a fleeting sign.
Melodies of unspoken words,
Sing of hopes like distant birds.

Curtains drawn to cloak the night,
Glimmers hint at what is right.
Sonatas in the quiet breeze,
Echo softly through the trees.

Every chord holds tight and close,
Binding longing in its dose.
In this dance of trust and fear,
We find solace, drawing near.

The Minor Key of Longing

In the dusk, emotions rise,
Crimson hues in twilight skies.
Longing lingers, sweet yet pain,
In the silence, love's refrain.

Melancholy notes softly weave,
Stories told in hearts that grieve.
Each heartbeat echoes, deep and low,
In minor keys, our feelings grow.

Yearning glances shared in vain,
Through the shadows, we remain.
Notes of sorrow, soft they blend,
Carrying whispers without end.

Fleeting moments, bittersweet,
In the space where lovers meet.
Holding on with fragile grace,
In the night, we seek our place.

Fugues of Friendship

In the laughter, bonds we find,
Harmony in heart and mind.
Fugues of joy play through our days,
In simple moments, love displays.

Together we create the sound,
In every glance, our joy is found.
Notes of trust that rise and fall,
A symphony that weaves through all.

With each challenge, hand in hand,
We compose a steady band.
Melodies of shared delight,
In every struggle, hearts ignite.

Through the years, our song remains,
Marking highs and soft refrains.
Fugues of friendship, bright and clear,
In unity, we persevere.

Overture of Trust

In the dawn, we build our way,
Notes of courage start to play.
Overtures that bind us tight,
In the glow of morning light.

As we move, we find our song,
In this space, we both belong.
Trusting hearts in every beat,
Creating music, bittersweet.

In the silence, strength we share,
A symphony beyond compare.
Every note, a promise made,
In our trust, no fears invade.

Together we face what may come,
In each challenge, we are one.
Overture of hope and grace,
In this journey, we embrace.

Lullabies of Longing

In the hush of twilight glow,
Whispers of dreams begin to flow.
Silent wishes ride the breeze,
Carried soft, like rustling leaves.

Stars awaken, one by one,
Softly smiling at the sun.
In the night, our hearts will dance,
Cradled close in sweet romance.

Every heartbeat, every sigh,
Promises made beneath the sky.
In this world, we drift and sway,
Lost in love, we fade away.

Moonlight wraps us in its plea,
Time stands still, just you and me.
Echoes linger, soft and clear,
Lullabies that draw you near.

So close your eyes, let dreams take flight,
In the comfort of the night.
Here we'll find our secret space,
Lullabies with warm embrace.

Rhythm of Togetherness

In the morning's golden hue,
Every moment feels so new.
Hand in hand we stride along,
Hearts entwined in hopeful song.

Every laugh, a spark of light,
In your gaze, the world feels right.
With each pulse, we sync our hearts,
In this dance, we'll never part.

Through the highs and through the lows,
In this bond, the love just grows.
Every challenge, side by side,
In your arms, I want to bide.

Life's a rhythm, soft and sweet,
Every heartbeat, every beat.
In the echoes, we shall find,
All the love that's intertwined.

Together we will write our tale,
Through the storms, we will not pale.
In this journey, come what may,
You and I will find our way.

Symphony of Sensations

The world awakens, colors gleam,
A vibrant dance, a living dream.
All around, the senses play,
A symphony in bright array.

The laughter mingles with the breeze,
Scent of flowers, sweet and free.
Every heartbeat strikes a chord,
A melody that can't be ignored.

With the sunlight's warm embrace,
We find joy in every space.
A gentle touch, a whispered word,
In this music, love is stirred.

Through the rustle of the leaves,
Nature sings, the heart believes.
Filling souls, this symphony,
We become what we can't see.

In the stillness, listen close,
Feel the rhythm, joy engross.
Every moment, every sound,
A symphony in love profound.

Crescendo of Dreams

In the silence, dreams take flight,
Soaring high in the velvet night.
Every wish a note in tune,
Dancing softly with the moon.

Climbing higher, we embrace,
Every heartbeat finds its place.
In this harmony we weave,
Moments cherished, we believe.

With each sunrise, hopes arise,
Painting futures in the skies.
Every dream a color bright,
Filling hearts with pure delight.

As our visions intertwine,
In this rhythm, you are mine.
Through the echoes, we shall hear,
Crescendo building, drawing near.

Let the music guide our way,
In this dance of night and day.
Here's our promise, love will bloom,
In the crescendo, find our room.

Melody Found in You

In whispers soft, your voice does sing,
A serenade that makes hearts spring.
Each note a treasure, pure and true,
In every chord, I find you too.

Through twilight's glow, we dance in time,
Two souls entwined, a perfect rhyme.
With every heartbeat, love's refrain,
In harmony, we share the pain.

The world fades out, just us remain,
A melody that breaks the chain.
In every breath, I feel the tune,
A symphony beneath the moon.

So let the music lead us on,
In every dusk, in every dawn.
For in this song, I find my place,
With you, my heart, my saving grace.

Harmonic Convergence

When stars align in skies so bright,
Two lives connect, a pure delight.
The universe hums a sacred song,
In this embrace, we both belong.

Voices blend like colors bright,
Creating a canvas, a wondrous sight.
Together we rise, never apart,
A duo crafted from one heart.

The rhythm swells with every sigh,
As dreams take flight like birds on high.
In every whisper, secrets stray,
An echo dances, come what may.

In the stillness, love's chorus breathes,
Binding us close like golden leaves.
Together we face the world anew,
In harmonic convergence, just me and you.

Rhapsody of the Heart

With gentle strokes, you paint my soul,
A rhapsody that makes me whole.
In every glance, a vivid hue,
A masterpiece, composed of you.

The symphony of laughter rings,
As love weaves in the joy it brings.
Each heartbeat drums a joyful start,
Creating echoes in the heart.

A waltz of memories, soft and sweet,
In every step, two hearts will meet.
The dance of time, a swirling grace,
In every turn, I find my place.

Through storms and sun, we'll sway and glide,
In rhapsody, forever side by side.
With every note, a promise swears,
In melodies, love always cares.

Interlude of Intimacy

Beneath the stars, we find our peace,
In quiet moments, all worries cease.
The world may spin, but here we lie,
In whispered dreams, just you and I.

Each tender touch, a spark ignites,
In shadows deep, our love invites.
With gentle warmth, our spirits blend,
In this interlude, hearts transcend.

The silence sings a sweet refrain,
A bond unbroken, love's domain.
In every heartbeat, secrets bloom,
A tender light in the darkest room.

As time stands still, we lose all fears,
In this embrace, we melt in tears.
With every breath, our souls take flight,
In intimate bliss, we find our light.

The Songbird's Tale

A songbird sings at break of dawn,
Its melodies weave through the air,
With notes that dance, a soothing balm,
In gentle whispers, it lays bare.

Through branches green, it flits and flies,
Chasing the light, the warm sunrise,
Each trill a tale of love and strife,
In every key, it finds new life.

The breeze carries its heartfelt tune,
Across the fields, beneath the moon,
It hums of joy, of loss, of hope,
In nature's arms, it learns to cope.

When night falls soft, it twinkles bright,
Upon the stars, it takes its flight,
A serenade to hearts so bold,
In dreams, its stories are retold.

So let it sing, this songbird free,
In every heart, its song shall be,
A timeless echo that will prevail,
Forever known as the songbird's tale.

Nocturne for Two

In twilight's grasp, two souls align,
Beneath the glow of silver light,
With hands entwined, a soft design,
They share a dance, a breath of night.

Their hearts converse in whispered tones,
Each note a promise, softly made,
In gentle hush, the world condones,
A sacred space where fears now fade.

Stars above begin to gleam,
As shadows twine and blush arise,
In this embrace, they find the dream,
Where silence speaks and love complies.

The moonlight paints their tender glow,
As melodies of night unfurl,
In every glance, the love they sow,
Two souls ignited, heartbeats whirl.

So as the night draws ever near,
They linger on, as lovers do,
In perfect harmony, they steer,
A nocturne soft, their love, so true.

Overture of Devotion

In quiet moments, true hearts meet,
A symphony of vows exchanged,
With every glance, a tender beat,
An overture, their lives arranged.

Through trials faced and joys embraced,
They tread the path of time together,
In storms and sun, their love's encased,
A bond that weathers any weather.

Each note they play, a promise cast,
In harmonies of trust and care,
With every echo, love holds fast,
In whispered tales, forever shared.

As seasons turn and years unfold,
Their dance of life, a wondrous sight,
In every heartbeat, stories told,
An overture that shines so bright.

So let the music softly rise,
A testament to hearts in tune,
For in devotion, love defies,
The world, a stage, their hearts a boon.

Flourish of Affection

In gardens lush, where colors bloom,
Two lovers stroll beneath the sun,
With laughter sweet, they chase the gloom,
In every step, their joy's begun.

The petals soft, the fragrance rare,
Embrace the warmth of love's allure,
With every glance, a tender care,
A flourish found, a heart so pure.

There's magic spun in each shared glance,
As butterflies lend grace to air,
In nature's grand and vibrant dance,
Their souls entwined in love's sweet snare.

Through sunlit paths and shaded trees,
They forge a bond, a timeless thread,
In every sigh, a gentle breeze,
A promise kept, a life ahead.

So let affection rise and swell,
Like blooms that greet the morning light,
In every heart, a story to tell,
A flourish bright, a love in flight.

Nocturne of the Heart

In twilight's gentle arms we sway,
Whispers of dreams in soft ballet.
Stars above in silence gleam,
Carrying the warmth of a secret theme.

The nightingale sings a tender tune,
Beneath the watchful gaze of the moon.
With every note our spirits soar,
In this serenade, we ask for more.

Shadows dance in rhythmic grace,
As hearts converge in this sacred space.
Embers glow in the fading light,
Binding souls in the heart of the night.

Soft echoes of laughter, sweet and light,
Embraced within the arms of night.
Every heartbeat's tender call,
A symphony that enchants us all.

In moonlit dreams, our secrets kept,
With every sigh, the world is swept.
In this nocturne, we find our rest,
Two souls entwined, forever blessed.

The Rhythm of You

In every heartbeat, I find the beat,
A melody of moments when our eyes meet.
The world may spin in a dizzy dance,
But in your gaze, I find my chance.

Soft whispers echo in the night,
A serenade where all feels right.
Each laugh we share a precious note,
Together we float on love's soft boat.

With every step, we find our way,
In the rhythm of love, we learn to sway.
The pulse of life, a delicate song,
With you by my side, I feel so strong.

In twilight's glow, our shadows blend,
A perfect harmony that will not end.
In gentle moments, our spirits fuse,
A timeless dance, in love we choose.

Every heartbeat, a whispered vow,
In this sweet rhythm, we live the now.
In the cadence of us, forever true,
I find my home, my rhythm in you.

Soundscapes of the Soul

In quiet corners, whispers sigh,
A symphony beneath the sky.
The rustling leaves in twilight's glow,
Compose a tune that gently flows.

With every breeze, a story sings,
The laughter of life in gentle rings.
Through valleys deep and mountains high,
The soundscapes echo, never shy.

In rivers' song and nature's hum,
A chorus rises, becomes the drum.
The heartbeat of earth, a wondrous grace,
Within this silence, I find my place.

As stars begin to twinkle bright,
The universe sings in the quiet night.
Each glimmer, a note in night's embrace,
Together we drift through time and space.

In this vast expanse, the soul's delight,
Every sound a spark, igniting the night.
With every breath, I become whole,
In the harmony found within my soul.

Moonlit Harmonies

In the silver glow of the night,
Soft shadows dance, a tender sight.
Underneath the starry dome,
In moonlit harmonies, we find our home.

A gentle breeze carries a tune,
Caressing us under the watchful moon.
Every whisper is a lullaby,
In this embrace, we soar and fly.

The echoes of love fill the air,
In each sweet moment, nothing compares.
With heartbeats soft and spirits free,
In this melody, it's just you and me.

Our dreams entwined in silver threads,
As stars above dance like our dreads.
Every sigh a note of bliss,
In moonlit harmonies, I find your kiss.

Together we weave the night's refrain,
A tapestry of love in joy and pain.
In this serenade, we've found our part,
In the symphony of our beating heart.

A Harmony Unbroken

In gentle whispers, hearts collide,
A dance of souls, where love resides.
Beneath the stars, we find our way,
In every note, our spirits sway.

Through storms and trials, we hold tight,
With every heartbeat, pure delight.
Together strong, we'll face the night,
A symphony that feels so right.

With each embrace, a tune is spun,
We share the warmth, two lives as one.
In laughter's glow, in silence, grace,
A perfect blend, our secret place.

As time unfolds, our song will soar,
Each melody opens a new door.
In harmony, we'll cast a spell,
With every breath, we know it well.

Melodic Bonds

Two voices merge in sweet refrain,
In shared dreams, we break the chain.
With every laugh, a chord we strike,
Our hearts compose what words can't write.

The rhythm flows, our pulses beat,
In every glance, the world feels sweet.
From dusk till dawn, we sing our song,
United in a love so strong.

Each note we share, a woven thread,
In symphony, our fears are shed.
With open hearts, we embrace the sound,
In this sweet harmony, we're found.

Through years to come, our melody,
A song of life, of you and me.
In every challenge, note, or chord,
Our love, the music we adored.

Prelude to Forever

In morning light, our eyes awake,
With gentle smiles, the dawn we take.
A whispered promise lingers near,
In every heartbeat, love sincere.

The world unfolds beneath our feet,
Each step we take, a rhythmic beat.
In every touch, a spark ignites,
A prelude to our wondrous nights.

We chart the course, our sails are high,
With hope as vast as the endless sky.
In every moment, magic grows,
A symphony that only we know.

As time flows on, we'll write our song,
In every heartbeat, where we belong.
With every breath, our tale begins,
In love's embrace, we'll always win.

The Art of Affection

In tender strokes, we paint our love,
A canvas bright, like skies above.
With every kiss, we shape the hue,
In softest colors, me and you.

With every word, a line we draw,
In mutual trust, we find our law.
Emotions blend, a masterpiece,
In love's great art, we find our peace.

Through gentle gestures, we create,
An endless dance that won't abate.
In quiet moments, beauty shines,
A work of heart, where love entwines.

In shades of joy, in strokes of pain,
We find our way through sun and rain.
In every heartbeat, art we share,
A timeless bond, beyond compare.

The Cadence of Caress

In whispers soft, we sway,
A dance of light at break of day.
Your touch ignites a gentle spark,
Illuminating paths through dark.

With every heartbeat, we entwine,
A rhythm sweet, a love divine.
Through tender sighs, our souls collide,
In your embrace, I find my guide.

Like petals falling in the breeze,
Each caress brings me to my knees.
A symphony of skin on skin,
In this cadence, we begin.

The world around us fades away,
As laughter lingers, here we stay.
In the warmth of your embrace,
I find my heart, my sacred space.

With every glance, we share the view,
In the rhythm of me and you.
A tender touch, a silent word,
In this moment, love is heard.

Orchestrating Our Journey

With maps unrolled upon the floor,
We chart our course for a new shore.
Each heartbeat sets a steady pace,
Together we will find our place.

Through valleys vast and mountains high,
With hands entwined, we'll touch the sky.
A symphony made of dreams and hope,
In unity, we learn to cope.

The road may twist, the winds may wail,
Yet side by side, we shall not fail.
For every chord that life may play,
We'll harmonize along the way.

In laughter's echoed, joyful shout,
We face the storms and cast out doubt.
With every step, our spirits soar,
Together, dear, we'll seek for more.

As night descends and stars ignite,
We weave our dreams within the light.
With courage found in love's embrace,
We orchestrate our destined place.

A Rhapsody of Resilience

In shadows cast by trials we face,
We rise again, we find our place.
With every tear, a seed is sown,
In fertile ground, new strength has grown.

The symphony of life may sway,
But hearts united find a way.
In every storm, a lesson learned,
With brighter days, our spirits turned.

Hear now the chords of courage sung,
In every note, our hearts are strung.
With hope as our unfailing guide,
We stand together, side by side.

In moments dark, when doubts arise,
We'll chase the light that never dies.
With laughter's grace, we'll pave the way,
In rhapsody, we find our stay.

The echoes of our journey strong,
In resilience, we all belong.
For through the fire, we shall glow,
In every heart, our strength will grow.

Symphony in Solitude

In quietude, my heart finds peace,
A symphony where worries cease.
The stillness wraps like velvet night,
In solitude, I find my light.

With whispered thoughts, I greet the day,
Each note a mindful, soft ballet.
As nature sings its gentle tune,
I dance beneath the silver moon.

The echoes of my soul resound,
In solitude, true self is found.
Through pages turned, my spirit soars,
In moments quiet, wisdom pours.

With every breath, a melody,
In solitary reverie.
The world outside may fade away,
Yet in this space, I'm here to stay.

In harmony with my own heart,
From solitude, I shall not part.
For in this symphony I see,
The beauty found in simply me.

Notes of Passion

In whispers soft, our secrets flow,
A melody only we can know.
Each heartbeat chimes, a vibrant tune,
Underneath the watchful moon.

Fingers trace the notes we play,
A symphony that won't decay.
With every breath, the sound grows bold,
A story of our love retold.

The tempo rises, hearts entwined,
In this dance, our souls aligned.
Across the canvas, colors blend,
In this harmony, we transcend.

Crimson roses in the night,
Glow like stars, our love's pure light.
Each moment sings, a cherished song,
Together where we both belong.

In every note, a spark ignites,
A passion that ignites the nights.
The world around us fades away,
Lost in the music, here we stay.

The Dance of Two Souls

In twilight's glow, two shadows merge,
A gentle sway, a tender surge.
The world retreats, it fades from view,
Just you and I, in steps so true.

Whispers echo, soft and clear,
Every heartbeat, drawing near.
With every twirl, our spirits rise,
Underneath the velvet skies.

The rhythm guides our hearts to beat,
In perfect time, we find our feet.
Together we glide, no end in sight,
Wrapped in the warmth of the night.

In laughter shared, in looks that spark,
We paint our love, create a mark.
A dance of dreams, where we belong,
Two souls entwined, forever strong.

As dawn approaches, we hold tight,
In this embrace, our love ignites.
No greater joy, no higher goal,
Than this sweet dance of two souls whole.

A Lullaby for Us

Close your eyes, my dear tonight,
Let the stars be our guiding light.
In the hush, a gentle breeze,
Sings a lullaby through the trees.

Dreams will carry us away,
To places where our hearts can play.
In every whisper, in every sigh,
Love's soft embrace will never die.

Moonbeams dance upon your face,
In this quiet, sacred space.
With every heartbeat, love will flow,
A tender bond that only grows.

Every star a wish we share,
In this moment, free of care.
With you, my heart will always stay,
Through night's embrace, we drift away.

So rest your head upon my chest,
In this lullaby, we are blessed.
Together safe, together free,
In love's embrace, just you and me.

Interludes of Intimacy

In quiet corners, where shadows play,
We find our words in whispers sway.
With every look, a story we tell,
An interlude where hearts swell.

Fingers lace in the softest touch,
In moments shared, we feel so much.
A breath, a sigh, the world fades out,
In this closeness, there's no doubt.

The soft glow of the fading light,
Wraps us up in its warm delight.
In silence, we speak a thousand dreams,
As love flows softly in gentle streams.

Each heartbeat echoes, a pulsating rhyme,
In this space, we stretch our time.
A dance of joy, of love's embrace,
In these interludes, we find our place.

So let the world spin and twirl,
We are a universe, you and I, girl.
In these moments, our spirits soar,
With each whisper, I love you more.

Heartfelt Reverberations

In the quiet of the night,
Whispers dance on silver light.
Echoes of a tender sigh,
Love's sweet song will never die.

Fingers trace the memories,
Carved in time like ancient trees.
Each pulse a gentle reminder,
Of hearts forever intertwined.

With every beat, the world fades,
As our own harmony cascades.
Melodies so pure and clear,
Playing only for each ear.

Underneath the starry skies,
Promises in soft replies.
Binding dreams in rhythmic flows,
Where the heart's true music grows.

Together we will find our way,
In this dance, where shadows play.
Every note a step we take,
Heartfelt echoes never break.

Dreaming in D Minor

In twilight's soft embrace we dream,
Notes floating like a quiet stream.
Chords that weave through endless skies,
Where hopes drift like the fireflies.

A melody of whispered fears,
Plays softly, soothing hidden tears.
With every sound, a tale unfolds,
Past ambitions, both young and bold.

D Minor holds a certain grace,
In every beat, a kept embrace.
The heartstrings pull with every tune,
Beneath the watchful crescent moon.

As shadows cast their fleeting glow,
The music leads where dreamers go.
Each note a step toward the light,
Cradled within the arms of night.

In harmony, our spirits soar,
Unlocking every hidden door.
In melodies, the silence breaks,
As dreamers dance for love's own sake.

Composed in Your Presence

In this space, where time stands still,
Each breath a note, a gentle thrill.
With every glance, a symphony,
Composed in pure serenity.

Your laughter paints the air with gold,
A timeless tale waiting to be told.
In silence, harmony resides,
Where tender secrets softly hide.

Like rivers flow, our spirits meet,
In every heart, a steady beat.
Together crafting what is true,
An opus born in shades of blue.

With every word, we shape the night,
In shadows danced with pale moonlight.
The world around us fades away,
As music forms the words we say.

In your gaze, I find my song,
Where all our notes have lived so long.
Composed in love, we'll never tire,
As heartstrings spark a lasting fire.

The Ballad of Us

Once upon a time we met,
Two souls entwined without regret.
Our story penned by stars above,
In every line, the threads of love.

Through stormy nights and sunny days,
We wandered through life's winding maze.
Hand in hand, we faced it all,
Together we would rise or fall.

With laughter's ring, we danced through time,
Each moment cherished, pure, sublime.
In whispered dreams, our secrets shared,
A bond that only we have dared.

We built a world of fleeting grace,
In every heartbeat, we found our place.
Like melodies that know no end,
In life's grand symphony, we blend.

So here's to all that lies ahead,
The paths we'll walk, the words we've said.
In this ballad, forever more,
Our love, the song we all adore.

Whispered Chords

In shadows soft, the notes arise,
A gentle hum beneath the skies.
Whispers shared, they drift away,
In quiet hearts, they long to stay.

Fingers dance on strings of night,
Carving dreams in silver light.
Every touch, a silent plea,
A melody that dares to be.

In the stillness, voices blend,
Echoes of what time can mend.
In every chord, a moment's grace,
A sacred space, a warm embrace.

Beneath the stars, where shadows play,
A tune unfolds, then fades away.
Yet in our hearts, it lingers long,
A whispered chord, forever strong.

The Unwritten Sonata

A song untold, in silence waits,
Each note a sigh, as fate dictates.
Ink yet to touch the papered thoughts,
In a world where memory rots.

Winds of change will softly stir,
The heart's own beat, they gently blur.
A symphony yet to be born,
In whispered dreams, new hopes are worn.

The dance of time, in soft embrace,
Uncharted paths, lost in space.
Each pause, a breath, a thought untold,
In this unwritten, brave and bold.

When shadows flee, and light returns,
We'll breathe in notes, and passion burns.
In harmony, we'll find our way,
The unwritten sonata will play.

Echoes of Embrace

In twilight's glow, we share a breath,
An echo's tale of life and death.
Fingers intertwined in silent song,
In this moment, we both belong.

Whispers linger like gentle waves,
In every glance, the heart enslaves.
Beneath the stars, we find our truth,
In the echoes, we reclaim youth.

The world outside begins to fade,
As time stands still, our fears betrayed.
In every heartbeat, love sustains,
A dance of shadows, joy remains.

We weave our dreams, like threads of gold,
In soft embraces, brave and bold.
Though echoes fade, the love won't cease,
In whispered vows, we find our peace.

Radiance in Dissonance

Amidst the clash of vibrant sounds,
The beauty lies where chaos bounds.
In dissonance, a truth unveiled,
A symphony of hearts derailed.

Unraveled notes collide and fall,
Yet in the storm, we heed the call.
For in the clash, we breathe in deep,
A melody that wakes from sleep.

Darkness meets the spark of light,
In every struggle, fierce and bright.
Through stubborn hearts, the music flows,
In dissonance, the radiance grows.

Together we'll rise, fierce and strong,
In the wild dance where we belong.
For every note that breaks apart,
Shall lead us back to the beating heart.

Harmonies of the Soul

In the quiet of the night,
Whispers float on moonlit air.
Hearts dance to soft delight,
Dreams weave songs, so rare.

Gentle breezes carry tunes,
Lifting spirits, free and light.
Melodies like silver moons,
Guide us through the night.

In the stillness, voices blend,
Echoes of a sacred place.
Where love's chorus has no end,
Time slows in its embrace.

Notes entwine in blissful sway,
Each heartbeat plays its part.
Harmonies that softly play,
Resonate within the heart.

Together we find our way,
A symphony of the soul.
With each note, come what may,
We become completely whole.

A Serenade in Starlight

Beneath a velvet, shining dome,
Stars twinkle with a soft caress.
Each light, a whisper from home,
A promise of sweet tenderness.

The nightingale sings her song,
Melodies that call the moon.
In this moment, we belong,
Hearts in rhythm, all too soon.

Waves of silver, dreams take flight,
Painted skies, a canvas vast.
Every twinkle, pure delight,
Reminds us of our shared past.

With every breath, the world slows,
Captured in this starlit trance.
Where love's magic surely grows,
A timeless, enchanted dance.

As shadows blend with dawn's first light,
We hold the memories tight.
In the serenade's sweet night,
Our souls forever take flight.

Echoes of Desire

In twilight's glow, the shadows play,
Echoes call from far away.
Whispers linger on the breeze,
Yearning hearts that long to please.

Each promise lies beneath the stars,
Fleeting wishes, hidden scars.
Desire dances; sparks ignite,
Within the depths of darkened night.

Moments fade, yet feelings grow,
Captured in the afterglow.
With every sigh, the silence swells,
A tale that only longing tells.

In these shadows, truths unfold,
Secrets shared, emotions bold.
Together, we vacate the night,
Searching for that flicker of light.

Grant me refuge in your gaze,
Where desire thrives and never sways.
Through echoes both fierce and sweet,
Our hearts will harmonize, complete.

Rhythms that Bind

In every heartbeat lies a song,
The pulse of life, steady and strong.
With every step, a dance begins,
A timeless tune where love spans thin.

Through joys and sorrows, we will sway,
Finding grace in every fray.
Together, we weave our thread,
In rhythms that softly spread.

With hands entwined, we'll chase the sun,
Laughing as the day is spun.
In whispers shared and glances bright,
We find our way through day and night.

The world may shift, the seasons change,
Yet through it all, our hearts exchange.
In every note, our souls combine,
Creating paths where love will shine.

As long as we embrace the beat,
In life's grand dance, we are complete.
These rhythms that forever bind,
A cherished love, forever kind.

The Pulse of Passion

In shadows deep, desire stirs,
A flame ignites, as silence blurs.
With whispered dreams, our hearts collide,
In every beat, our souls reside.

The moonlight dances on the floor,
A rhythm strong, we crave for more.
Each touch a spark, electric, bright,
Our universe, consumed by light.

Through woven paths, our spirits soar,
In tangled threads, we dare explore.
With every glance, a story told,
In passion's grasp, our hearts unfold.

Time slips away, a fleeting breeze,
Yet in this moment, we find ease.
The pulse of love, a steady drum,
In perfect harmony, we hum.

Together lost, forever found,
In whispered dreams, we stand our ground.
With every breath, the world stands still,
In love's embrace, we feel the thrill.

A canvas bright, our colors mix,
In this wild dance, a perfect fix.
With every heartbeat, we ignite,
The pulse of passion, pure delight.

Enchanted Echoes

In twilight's glow, where shadows play,
The echoes call, they gently sway.
Through forest whispers, secrets weave,
Enchanted tales for hearts to believe.

A symphony of rustling leaves,
In every note, a magic weaves.
The world transforms with every sound,
In nature's arms, we're closely bound.

Beneath the stars, the night unfolds,
With shimmering lights, the silence holds.
Each star a wish, a guiding light,
In enchanted echoes of the night.

Dreams take flight on gentle wings,
In melodies, our spirit sings.
With every breath, the night profound,
In whispered hopes, our love is found.

The shadows dance, the night conspires,
To kindle softly our heart's desires.
As echoes fade, a promise stays,
In heart's embrace, forever plays.

Heartstrings Entwined

Two souls converge on a winding road,
Each step we take, a shared abode.
With laughter sweet, our journey starts,
In tender space, we bind our hearts.

A tapestry of dreams unfurls,
In every twist, our love unfurls.
Through seasons change, we stand as one,
In gentle whispers, our hopes begun.

With every glance, a spark ignites,
In deepest night, our hearts take flight.
We weave the threads of joy and pain,
In every tear, our love remains.

In sunlight's glow, we find our way,
Through stormy skies, come what may.
With hands held tight, we're intertwined,
In sacred dance, our dreams aligned.

As time ticks on, our bond won't break,
With every heartbeat, memories make.
In harmony, with feelings twined,
Forever yours, our hearts aligned.

Ethereal Resonance

In softest light, the dawn breaks clear,
A melody that draws us near.
With whispers sweet, the morning sings,
In ethereal waves, our spirit clings.

The colors blend, a canvas bright,
In each brushstroke, love takes flight.
Across the skies, our dreams cascade,
In harmony's arms, we're unafraid.

With every wave, the ocean swells,
A timeless tale that nature tells.
In gentle rhythms, we are bound,
In each embrace, pure love is found.

As twilight falls, we chase the stars,
With every wish, our dreams are ours.
In cosmic dance, our hearts align,
An ethereal resonance divine.

Through endless nights, our souls will roam,
In every heartbeat, we find home.
With love's embrace, we shall ascend,
In cosmic light, our journeys blend.

Vibrations of Verity

In the stillness of the night,
Whispers of truth take flight.
Echoes dance with the stars,
Illuminating hidden scars.

Raindrops sing on rooftops high,
Melodies of the clouded sky.
Each sound a gentle plea,
For the heart to be set free.

Resonance of souls entwined,
In every note, a story lined.
The rhythm of life's embrace,
Guides us to our rightful place.

Waves of courage wash ashore,
With every chord, we seek for more.
In unison, we rise and fall,
Answering the universe's call.

Together we dance, not alone,
In harmony, we've grown to own.
Vibrations of verity ring clear,
In the silence, we persevere.

The Heart's Labyrinth

Winding paths of passion's maze,
Each turn holds a different phase.
Echoes of love lost and found,
In shadows where dreams abound.

Every corner holds a sigh,
Whispered secrets, reasons why.
A lingering touch, a fleeting glance,
In this world, we take our chance.

Twists and turns, the journey's long,
In hearts where we both belong.
Through the darkness, we find light,
Guided by the stars at night.

A beacon calling me to stay,
In this labyrinth, come what may.
With every step, the heart beats loud,
Wrapped in the love we found.

Together we navigate the maze,
Lost and found in love's warm gaze.
In tangled paths, we redefine,
The heart, a precious, sacred shrine.

Whispered Harmonies

In the still air, a soft refrain,
Notes of love brush against the rain.
Each melody, a gentle thread,
Stitching dreams where we were led.

Fingers dancing across the keys,
Creating symphonies with ease.
A whispered song of hope and light,
Guiding us through the darkest night.

Swaying gently, hearts aligned,
In this moment, love defines.
Echoes linger, warm and sweet,
In whispered harmonies, we meet.

With every chord, a promise made,
A beautiful serenade.
Together, we can find our way,
Through the music, come what may.

Let the world fade away outside,
In these notes, there's naught to hide.
Whispered harmonies arise,
A symphony beneath the skies.

Love Letters in Melody

Ink spills over parchment bare,
Each stroke a longing, a silent prayer.
Love letters wrapped in melody,
Composing a timeless symphony.

In the quiet, words unfold,
Stories of warmth in tales retold.
With every line, a heartbeat flows,
A garden of emotion grows.

Verses bloom, sweet fragrance ripe,
In each stanza, a loving type.
Whispers carried on the breeze,
A written tune that puts us at ease.

Secrets shared in notes and rhymes,
Echoes caught in passing times.
In the dance of pen and page,
We find the wisdom of our age.

Let us ink the skies with song,
In every line, we all belong.
Love letters linger in the air,
Melodies beyond compare.

Stringing Together Moments

We gather our fragments, each one a find,
Hidden in laughter, where stories unwind.
With threads made of memories, we sew,
  Creating a tapestry, vibrant and slow.

Each whisper a bead, each glance a stone,
  Crafted with care, together alone.
The colors of joy blend with shades of fear,
Stringing together moments we hold dear.

Time dances lightly, a soft serenade,
In the garden of now, where shadows fade.
With hands intertwined, we chase twilight's glow,
Stringing together moments, the heart's true show.

Like jewels in a crown, each one so bright,
Moments shine clearer in the soft, dim light.
An orchestra plays, each note in our chest,
Stringing together times when we felt blessed.

So let us not rush, but relish the lane,
In the chorus of laughter, the echo of pain.
Together we weave, let the tales ignite,
Stringing together moments, weaving through night.

The Tones of Together

In shadows we linger, in daylight we play,
Finding the rhythm in each passing day.
The tones of our laughter, the sighs and the hums,
Together we rise, where harmony comes.

A symphony built of both joy and of tears,
In the dance of our lives, we lighten our fears.
With notes intertwined, our hearts beat in time,
The tones of together, a beautiful rhyme.

When silence surrounds us, it whispers so sweet,
In the pauses and spaces, our souls gently meet.
Together we listen, to music so low,
The tones of our being, a soft, steady flow.

With hands clasped in union, we chart a new song,
The melody strong, and yet tender along.
Each moment a note, every glance a refrain,
The tones of together break through the mundane.

So let us embrace this resounding embrace,
With love as our compass, no fear can we face.
In the symphony played, let us endlessly sway,
The tones of together, forever at play.

Interplay of Intimacy

In the quiet corners, where whispers reside,
The interplay glimmers, where hearts open wide.
With every small gesture, our souls gently blend,
In moments of silence, intimacy's friend.

The brush of a hand, a glance that ignites,
In the tapestry woven, the thread of our sights.
Together we wander through shadows and light,
In the interplay's dance, everything feels right.

With laughter as fuel, and dreams as our guide,
The depth of our bond, we never confide.
In knowing each secret, we silently grow,
Interplay of intimacy, setting hearts aglow.

Each sigh a soft promise, each touch a sweet chance,
In a world filled with chaos, we find our own dance.
Through the storms that may come, we stand side by side,

In the interplay of warmth, our hearts will abide.

So here in this moment, let's treasure the space,
Where intimacy blossoms, and time leaves no trace.
With every soft murmur, every shared gaze,
Interplay of intimacy, our hearts set to blaze.

Sonnet in the Twilight

As dusk falls gently, painting skies with gold,
In twilight's embrace, our stories unfold.
With shadows that flicker, and stars peeking through,
A sonnet in moments, just me and you.

Each heartbeat a verse, every breath a refrain,
In the soft, fading light, we dance through the plain.
The world slips away as we weave through the night,
A sonnet in the twilight, a bond shining bright.

With whispers like petals, we craft what we're feeling,
In the hush of the hour, our dreams are revealing.
The beauty of silence, a comforting hand,
A sonnet in the twilight, where time will not stand.

So gather the moments, let memories flow,
In the light of the evening, where true lovers go.
The echoes of passion, soft shadows in view,
A sonnet in the twilight, forever with you.

As the stars start to flicker, and night claims the day,
We'll cherish this sonnet, in night's gentle sway.
For in every soft sigh, our hearts shall ignite,
A sonnet in the twilight, a love burning bright.

Chimes of Togetherness

In the breeze, soft whispers play,
Echoes dance through light of day.
Hands entwined, hearts beat as one,
Underneath the setting sun.

Memories woven, threads so bright,
In shadowed corners, new joys ignite.
Laughter rings, a melody sweet,
In every moment, love's heartbeat.

Every chime tells tales of old,
In warmth of hearts, new stories unfold.
Together we stand, come what may,
In the chimes that guide our way.

From dawn's glow to twilight's gleam,
We sail through life on love's shared dream.
Hand in hand, we face the night,
Chimes of joy, our guiding light.

With every note, our spirits rise,
In harmony beneath the skies.
United in rhythm, side by side,
Chimes of togetherness, our pride.

Timeless Tantrums

In the silence, tempests brew,
Hearts collide, emotions true.
Words like arrows, sharp and bright,
Pierce the darkness of the night.

Fractured dreams in shadows lie,
Screams like thunder fill the sky.
Yet in chaos, love can bloom,
From the shadows, break the gloom.

Raging storms can leave us sore,
But through the pain, we seek for more.
Lessons learned in angry fights,
Build a bridge to warm delights.

Time moves on, the storms will pass,
Sunshine breaks through hardened glass.
With each tantrum, a chance to mend,
In love's embrace, we find the end.

So let us clash, then softly heal,
In every storm, a pain concealed.
With every tear, a chance to see,
The timeless dance of you and me.

Love in the Key of Dream

In twilight's hue, we softly sway,
Melodies drift, then fade away.
A whispered wish upon the air,
In dreams we find what hearts declare.

Notes of laughter, echoes clear,
Hopes entwined, when you are near.
In the quiet, your voice hums,
A symphony in two, love comes.

Stars above, a canvas spread,
Paint our stories, hopes unfed.
Together we chase the night's allure,
In dreams, our souls forever pure.

Every chord ignites the spark,
Turning light into the dark.
With every glance, a waltz begins,
In the key of love, our journey spins.

As dawn arrives, the shades will lift,
Within the light, love's precious gift.
Though dreams may fade, our song remains,
In the key of love, our hearts sustain.

A Harp's Gentle Embrace

Strings in twilight, soft and low,
Whisper tales that ebb and flow.
Fingers dance on wood and wire,
Craft a lullaby of desire.

In every pluck, a secret sigh,
Notes like raindrops, cascading high.
Harmony wraps us, snug and tight,
In the warmth of the velvet night.

A symphony in moon's soft glow,
Each vibration, love's gentle show.
With every strum, a heartbeat finds,
The thread that weaves two hopeful minds.

Cradled in sound, we drift away,
In a world where we can play.
Each echo brings a sweet caress,
In a harp's gentle, loving dress.

So let us lie in music's grace,
In every note, a warm embrace.
A serenade, forever free,
In a harp's love, just you and me.

Euphony of Hearts

In the quiet of the night,
Two souls find their gentle spark.
Whispers dance like firelight,
Binding dreams within the dark.

Harmony flows through the air,
Every heartbeat sings a tune.
With you, life is rare and fair,
An everlasting monsoon.

Fingers intertwine like vines,
Roots entwined beneath the earth.
In each touch, a love that shines,
A testament to our worth.

Melodies flicker like stars,
Painting skies in shades divine.
Close are we, no distant bars,
Together, hearts forever align.

Symphony of fate declares,
Every note a love's embrace.
In this world where nothing dares,
We create our sacred space.

Whispering Melodies

Softly flowing through the trees,
Gentle breezes coax the leaves.
Nature sings with such sweet ease,
A lullaby that never leaves.

Echoes of your tender voice,
Bounce upon the moonlit lake.
In your gaze, my heart's rejoice,
Every moment, love's heartache.

Listen close to time's soft beat,
Every second made for two.
In the rhythm, love's deceit,
Transformation, pure and true.

Together, we compose our fate,
Chords of laughter intertwine.
In our hearts, no hint of hate,
Only whispers, yours and mine.

By your side, the world feels right,
Every silence tells a tale.
Whispered dreams take flight at night,
In this love, we shall prevail.

The Crescendo of Togetherness

Rising notes through night's embrace,
Build the foundation of our song.
In the light, we leave no trace,
Only echoes, proud and strong.

Time cascades like a waterfall,
Drowning fears, igniting hope.
In deep joy, we stand so tall,
With love, forever we elope.

Heartbeat's rhythm, pure and bright,
Guides us through this vibrant dance.
Hand in hand, we find our flight,
Lost in love's sweet, fervent trance.

As the melody ascends high,
Let the world fade from our sight.
Together, we will never die,
In the symphony of light.

In the end, like stars, we shine,
Casting shadows of our grace.
Crescendo forged by hearts entwined,
In each note, we find our place.

Chords of Affection

Gentle strums on heartstrings play,
Caressing souls with every touch.
In this moment, words can't say,
What we feel, it means so much.

Every glance, a melody,
Sung in whispers, pure delight.
In your arms, the world we see,
Glowing softly in the night.

Affection blooms like springtime flowers,
Coloring the canvas bright.
With you, love's magic showers,
Painting shadows with pure light.

Through life's trials, we'll compose,
Chords of laughter, joy, and tears.
In this journey, love only grows,
Dancing through the passing years.

So let our hearts in love's refrain,
Create a symphony of dreams.
Together, we shall break the chain,
Flowing freely like the streams.

Soprano of the Heart

In the silence where whispers dwell,
A melody begins to swell,
Notes of love upon the air,
Carrying secrets, sweet and rare.

With every rise, a heartbeat sings,
Softly woven, a tapestry of wings,
Breathless moments, held so tight,
A serenade beneath the night.

Echoes dance in the tender space,
Her voice, a gentle warm embrace,
Flowing like a river deep,
Awakening dreams from their sleep.

Every sigh, a symphony's claim,
Flickers of passion, igniting the flame,
In the core, where souls entwine,
A harmony rich, like vintage wine.

As the final note starts to fade,
In the heart, the magic laid,
Soprano soft, a lasting part,
Her song will always fill the heart.

Duet of Dreams

In twilight's glow, we start to weave,
Two hearts aligned, a chance to believe,
Voices blend, a sweet refrains,
In the dance of love, we find no chains.

Each whispered hope, a thread we share,
A canvas painted with wishes rare,
Hand in hand, beneath starlit skies,
Building castles where our spirits rise.

Every challenge, we face as one,
In the duet, our fears are undone,
Harmony flows in sweet embrace,
Dreams take flight, a boundless space.

Through valleys low and peaks so high,
Together we soar, never shy,
With laughter ringing, a joyful tune,
In the heart's gallery, love's art is strewn.

So let us sing, our souls unite,
In the echo of this pure delight,
For in this moment, love redeems,
As we belong in our duet of dreams.

The Ballad of Us

Under the stars, our story unfolds,
A ballad whispered, a tale retold,
Through seasons changing, love remains,
In every joy and all the pains.

Every glance, a chapter starts,
Binding together our tender hearts,
In laughter shared and tears that fall,
We find strength through it all.

Through winds of change, we'll stand as one,
Facing the storms, until the sun,
Guides our path with radiant light,
Holding each other through the night.

Memories like rivers flow,
Together we rise, together we grow,
In the silence of knowing smiles,
Our love conquers the trials and miles.

So here we stand, in this embrace,
Writing our ballad, a timeless space,
With every verse, the truth sings clear,
The ballad of us, forever near.

Crescendos of Connection

In the quiet, a spark ignites,
A crescendo we feel in the nights,
Every heartbeat, a rhythm divine,
Closer we draw, our souls align.

Through whispers shared, our worlds collide,
A melody born, where love abides,
Notes entwine in a sweet embrace,
A dance of shadows, a warming grace.

Each promise spoken, a gentle swell,
In the crescendos, we weave our spell,
Through valleys deep and mountains tall,
Together we rise, we'll never fall.

In the canvas of time, we paint our song,
With shades of hope where we belong,
Every moment, a symphony bright,
Illuminating our darkest night.

So let the music play on, rejoice,
In the crescendos, we find our voice,
Connected forever, no need for pretense,
Our hearts in union, pure recompense.

Serenade Under the Stars

In the night, whispers softly call,
Beneath the moon, we hear it all.
Stars above like diamonds shine,
As your hand gently rests in mine.

The breeze carries our dreams away,
With each breath, the shadows sway.
Melodies dance in silver light,
Wrapped in warmth, we find our flight.

Voices blend, a sweet refrain,
Hearts united, we feel no pain.
In this serenade, love's sweet kiss,
Together, we find eternal bliss.

Time stands still, the world is near,
In this moment, there's nothing to fear.
With every note, our souls entwine,
A symphony, forever divine.

As dawn breaks, the stars take flight,
Leaving us with morning's light.
Yet in our hearts, the song remains,
A serenade that never wanes.

Ballad of the Beloved

In shadows deep, your visage glows,
Like petals kissed by morning's prose.
A heart once lost, now found within,
Embracing love, where dreams begin.

Your laughter paints the dusk with light,
A melody that feels so right.
In every glance, a story told,
A treasure more than silver or gold.

Through trials faced, we stand as one,
Two souls together, battles won.
In the quiet, our whispers blend,
In the silence, love knows no end.

With every touch, a spark ignites,
In your embrace, the world ignites.
Time may fade, but hearts will sing,
Forever cherished, you are my spring.

So let us dance beneath the moon,
A timeless waltz, a sweetened tune.
For in this ballad, we belong,
In love's embrace, forever strong.

Tapestry of Tones

Threads of color, voices blend,
In harmony, the melodies send.
Each note weaves a story bright,
A tapestry that feels just right.

Rhythms pulse like a beating heart,
From chaos, we create our art.
In every strum, the soul reveals,
A richness only love can feel.

With gentle chords, we shape our fate,
In every play, emotions sate.
Together we build our song anew,
A masterpiece made just for two.

The strings vibrate with life's embrace,
In this dance, we find our place.
With every touch, creation flows,
In this tapestry, our love grows.

So let the music fill the air,
With every note, we find our care.
In this union, we shall thrive,
In the tapestry, we are alive.

Symphony of Embraces

In every hug, a warmth unfolds,
A secret language silently told.
Arms entwined, a sweet embrace,
In your love, I find my place.

With gentle sway, our bodies blend,
In every moment, pain will mend.
Together, we are music's flow,
A symphony only we know.

In quiet whispers, hopes take flight,
With every heartbeat, pure delight.
The world fades when you hold me near,
In your embrace, there's no more fear.

Underneath the sky's vast dome,
With you, I truly feel at home.
In this symphony, we compose,
Every note, our love bestows.

The evening ends, but we remain,
In memory, we'll dance again.
For in your arms, my heart will sing,
Forever held in love's sweet ring.

The Sound of Togetherness

In the gentle breeze we share,
Laughter dances through the air.
Hand in hand, we roam this land,
Together, we firmly stand.

In the glow of sunset's hue,
Every moment feels so true.
Whispers soft, a sweet caress,
In your smile, I feel blessed.

Hearts entwined, we face the day,
In your light, I find my way.
With each step, a bond we weave,
In this love, we both believe.

Through the storms and rainy skies,
We find peace as time complies.
In the rhythm of our beat,
Life unfolds, so warm and sweet.

With a trust that knows no end,
Every moment we transcend.
In the sound of joy, we sing,
Together, our hearts take wing.

Poetic Echoes

Whispers in the quiet night,
Words that shimmer, softly bright.
Every phrase, a stolen glance,
In the shadows, we embrace.

Tales of love, of loss, of grace,
Echo through this timeless space.
Each heartbeat sings a melody,
In this dance, we are set free.

Rhythms swell like ocean tides,
In the verses, truth abides.
From the past, we draw our ink,
In our stories, we shall think.

Like the stars that pierce the dark,
Every line ignites a spark.
Crafted dreams on paper flow,
In their depths, the mirrors glow.

Through the pages, we will roam,
In the poems, we find home.
Every echo tells a tale,
In the silence, we prevail.

Serene Harmonies

In the garden, soft and still,
Nature's whispers, gentle thrill.
Birds in chorus, skies of blue,
Every note feels fresh and new.

Breezes weave through leaves so green,
In this moment, pure and serene.
Melodies in twilight's glow,
Hearts in time, as rivers flow.

Mountains stand with timeless grace,
In their shadows, we find space.
Every echo, every sigh,
Sings of peace beneath the sky.

Moments wrapped in soft embrace,
In the silence, find your place.
With each heartbeat, worlds align,
In these harmonies, we shine.

Through the seasons, we will find,
Beauty held in heart and mind.
In the quiet, truths arise,
In each harmony, love lies.

Duet in the Twilight

As the sun bids soft farewell,
In the dusk, our stories swell.
Two voices blend in evening's glow,
In the twilight, love will flow.

Shadows dance on paths so bright,
In your eyes, the stars ignite.
With each note, our souls entwine,
In this moment, you are mine.

Whispers drift like petals fair,
In the silence, hearts declare.
Side by side, we share our dreams,
In each wish, a spark redeems.

As the world begins to fade,
Every memory we have made.
In the warmth of dusk's embrace,
We find time cannot erase.

With the moon, our duet soars,
In the night, love gently roars.
Through the stars, we hear the call,
In this night, we have it all.

Milton Keynes UK
Ingram Content Group UK Ltd.
UKHW02191528 1024
450365UK00017B/806